Brownie Coo

Delicious Homemade Brownie Recipes You Can Easily Make At Home!

Copyright ©

All rights reserved. No part of this book may be reproduced, stored in a retrieval system, or transmitted in any form or by any means, electronic, mechanical, photocopying, recording, scanning, or otherwise, without the prior written permission of the publisher.

Disclaimer

All the material contained in this book is provided for educational and informational purposes only. No responsibility can be taken for any results or outcomes resulting from the use of this material.

While every attempt has been made to provide information that is both accurate and effective, the author does not assume any responsibility for the accuracy or use/misuse of this information.

You should always consult a doctor regarding any medical conditions, the information in this book is not intended to diagnose or treat any medical condition or illness.

Table of Contents

Introduction

Chocolate Fudge Brownies

Caramel Chocolate Brownies

Apple Brownies

Blonde Brownies

Peanut Butter Brownies

Frosted Chocolate Brownies

Caramel Brownies

Applesauce Brownies

Marbled Peanut Butter Brownies

Marshmallow Brownies

Easy Cheesecake Brownies

Butterscotch Blondies

Chocolate Mint Brownies

Vanilla Brownies

Double Chocolate Chip Brownies

Peppermint Brownies

Walnut Chocolate Brownies

Cherry Cheesecake Brownies

Coconut Brownies

Coffee Brownies

Snickerdoodle Brownies

Coconut Cherry Brownies

Dark Chocolate Brownies

Macadamia Nut Brownies

Raspberry Walnut Brownies

Introduction

This cookbook includes a variety of unique and delicious brownie recipes that you can easily make at home. As a professional baker I have come across all kinds of brownie recipes, and I would like to share my favorite brownie recipes with you.

I have provided easy to follow steps with these recipes, so both beginner and novice bakers can make these fresh homemade brownies. These recipes were the most popular in my bakery, and I think you will really enjoy them!

Chocolate Fudge Brownies

Ingredients

3/4 cup unsweetened cocoa powder

1/2 teaspoon baking soda

1/3 cup vegetable oil

1/2 cup boiling water

2 cups white sugar

2 eggs

1/3 cup vegetable oil

1 1/3 cups all-purpose flour

1 teaspoon vanilla extract

1/4 teaspoon salt

Directions

Preheat oven to 350 F (175 degrees C). Grease and flour a 9x13 inch pan.

In a large bowl, stir together the cocoa and baking soda. Add 1/3 cup vegetable oil and boiling water. Mix until well blended and thickened. Stir in the sugar, eggs, and remaining 1/3 cup oil. Finally, add the flour, vanilla and salt; mix just until all of the flour is absorbed. Spread evenly into the prepared pan.

Bake in the preheated oven for 35 to 40 minutes, or until a toothpick inserted into the cake comes out clean. Allow to cool before cutting into squares.

Caramel Chocolate Brownies

Ingredients

14 ounces caramels

1/2 cup evaporated milk

1 (18.25 ounce) package chocolate cake mix

1/3 cup evaporated milk

3/4 cup butter, melted

1/4 cup chopped pecans

2 cups milk chocolate chips

Directions

Peel caramels and place in a microwave-safe bowl. Stir in 1/2 cup evaporated milk. Heat and stir until all caramels are melted.

Preheat oven to 350 degrees F (175 degrees C) Grease a 9x13 inch pan.

In a large mixing bowl, mix together cake mix, 1/3 cup evaporated milk, melted butter, and chopped pecans. Place 1/2 of the batter in prepared baking pan.

Bake for 8 minutes.

Place the remaining batter into the fridge. Remove brownies from oven and sprinkle chocolate chips on top.

Drizzle caramel sauce over chocolate chips. Remove brownie mix from refrigerator. Using a teaspoon, make small balls with the batter and smash flat. Very carefully, place on top of the caramel sauce until the top is completely covered.

Bake for an additional 20 minutes. Remove and let cool.

Apple Brownies

Ingredients

1/2 cup butter, melted

1 cup white sugar

1 egg

3 medium apples - peeled, cored and thinly sliced

1/2 cup chopped walnuts

1 cup all-purpose flour

1/4 teaspoon salt

1/2 teaspoon baking powder

1/2 teaspoon baking soda

1 teaspoon ground cinnamon

Directions

Preheat oven to 350 degrees F (175 degrees C). Grease a 9x9 inch baking dish.

In a large bowl, beat together the melted butter, sugar, and egg until fluffy. Fold in the apples and walnuts. In a separate bowl, sift together the flour, salt, baking powder, baking soda, and cinnamon. Stir the flour mixture into the wet mixture until just blended. Spread the batter evenly in the prepared baking dish.

Bake 35 minutes in the preheated oven, or until a toothpick inserted in the center comes out clean.

Blonde Brownies

Ingredients

1 cup sifted all-purpose flour

1/2 teaspoon baking powder

1/8 teaspoon baking soda

1/2 teaspoon salt

1/2 cup chopped walnuts

1/3 cup butter, melted

1 cup packed brown sugar

1 egg, beaten

1 tablespoon vanilla extract

2/3 cup semisweet chocolate chips

Directions

Preheat oven to 350 degrees F (180 degrees C). Grease a 9x9-inch baking pan.

Measure 1 cup sifted flour. Add baking powder, baking soda, and salt. Sift again. Add 1/2 cup chopped nuts. Mix well and set aside.

Stir the brown sugar into the melted butter and mix well. Cool slightly.

Mix the beaten egg and vanilla into the brown sugar mixture. Add flour mixture, a little at a time, mixing just until combined.

Spread the batter into the prepared pan. Sprinkle 1/2 to 1 cup chocolate chips on top. Bake in the preheated oven until a toothpick inserted in the center comes out clean, about 20 to 25 minutes.

Peanut Butter Brownies

Ingredients

1/2 cup peanut butter

1/3 cup margarine, softened

2/3 cup white sugar

1/2 cup packed brown sugar

2 egg

1/2 teaspoon vanilla extract

1 cup all-purpose flour

1 teaspoon baking powder

1/4 teaspoon salt

Directions

Preheat oven to 350 degrees F (175 degrees C). Grease a 9x9 inch baking pan.

In a medium bowl, cream together peanut butter and margarine. Gradually blend in the brown sugar, white sugar, eggs, and vanilla; mix until fluffy. Combine flour, baking powder, and salt; stir into the peanut butter mixture until well blended.

Bake for 30 to 35 minutes in preheated oven, or until the top springs back when touched. Cool, and cut into 16 squares.

Frosted Chocolate Brownies

Ingredients

1/2 cup butter

1 cup white sugar

2 eggs

1 teaspoon vanilla extract

1/3 cup unsweetened cocoa powder

1/2 cup all-purpose flour

1/4 teaspoon salt

1/4 teaspoon baking powder

Frosting:

3 tablespoons butter, softened

3 tablespoons unsweetened cocoa powder

1 tablespoon honey

1 teaspoon vanilla extract

1 cup confectioners' sugar

Directions

Preheat oven to 350 degrees F (175 degrees C). Grease and flour an 8-inch square pan.

In a large saucepan, melt 1/2 cup butter. Remove from heat, and stir in sugar, eggs, and 1 teaspoon vanilla. Beat in 1/3 cup cocoa, 1/2 cup flour, salt, and baking powder. Spread batter into prepared pan.

Bake in preheated oven for 25 to 30 minutes. Do not overcook.

To Make Frosting: Combine 3 tablespoons softened butter, 3 tablespoons cocoa, honey, 1 teaspoon vanilla extract, and 1 cup confectioners' sugar. Stir until smooth. Frost brownies while they are still warm.

Caramel Brownies

Ingredients
1 (14 ounce) package individually wrapped caramels

2/3 cup evaporated milk

1 (18.25 ounce) package chocolate cake mix

3/4 cup butter, melted

1 teaspoon vanilla extract

1 cup semisweet chocolate chips

1 cup chopped walnuts

Directions
Preheat oven to 350 degrees F (175 degrees C). Grease one 9x13 inch baking dish.

Melt caramels and 1/3 cup of the evaporated milk over very low heat, stirring occasionally until smooth.

Combine cake mix, melted butter, the remaining 1/3 cup evaporated milk, vanilla and nuts. Mix well and spread 1/2 of the batter into the prepared pan.

Bake at 350 degrees F (175 degrees C) for 8 minutes.

Sprinkle the chocolate chips evenly over the partially cooked brownies. Pour the melted caramel mixture over the top and with a teaspoon drop the remaining 1/2 of the batter evenly over the top.

Bake at 350 degrees F (175 degrees C) for 20 minutes. Let brownies cool in pan then cut into bars.

Applesauce Brownies

Ingredients

1 1/2 cups white sugar

1/2 cup margarine

2 eggs

2 tablespoons unsweetened cocoa powder

1 1/2 teaspoons salt

2 cups applesauce

1 teaspoon baking soda

1 teaspoon ground cinnamon

2 cups all-purpose flour

2 tablespoons white sugar

1 cup semisweet chocolate chips

1 cup chopped walnuts

Directions

Preheat oven to 350 degrees F (175 degrees C).

Cream 1 1/2 cups sugar and margarine. Add eggs. Sift cocoa, salt, baking soda, cinnamon and flour ingredients and add to sugar mixture, alternately with applesauce. Pour into 10-1/2 X 15-1/2 inch jelly roll pan.

Combine 2 tablespoon sugar, 1 cup chocolate chips and 1 cup chopped nuts. Sprinkle over batter. Bake for 30 minutes.

Marbled Peanut Butter Brownies

Ingredients

2 (3 ounce) packages cream cheese, softened

1/2 cup peanut butter

1/4 cup white sugar

1 egg

2 tablespoons milk

1 cup butter or margarine, melted

2 cups white sugar

2 teaspoons vanilla extract

3 eggs

3/4 cup unsweetened cocoa powder

1 1/4 cups all-purpose flour

1/2 teaspoon baking powder

1/4 teaspoon salt

1 cup semisweet chocolate chips

Directions

Preheat oven to 350 degrees F (175 degrees C). Grease one 9x13 inch baking pan.

In a medium bowl, beat cream cheese, peanut butter, 1/4 cup white sugar, 1 egg, and milk until smooth. Set aside.

In a large bowl, mix together melted butter, 2 cups white sugar, and vanilla. Mix in the remaining 3 eggs one at a time, beating well after each addition. Combine flour, cocoa, baking powder, and salt; mix into the batter. Stir in chocolate chips.

Remove 1 cup of the chocolate batter. Spread the remaining batter into the prepared pan. Spread the peanut butter filling over the top. Drop the reserved chocolate batter by teaspoonful over the filling. Using a knife, gently swirl through the top layers for a marbled effect.

Bake in preheated oven for 35 to 40 minutes, or until a wooden toothpick inserted near the center comes out almost clean. Cool completely, then cut into bars.

Marshmallow Brownies

Ingredients

1 cup butterscotch chips

1/2 cup butter

1 1/2 cups all-purpose flour

2/3 cup packed brown sugar

2 teaspoons baking powder

1/2 teaspoon salt

1 teaspoon vanilla extract

2 eggs

2 cups miniature marshmallows

2 cups milk chocolate chips

Directions

Preheat oven to 350 degrees F (175 degrees C). Lightly grease a 9x13 inch baking pan.

Melt butterscotch morsels and margarine in a large bowl in microwave. Stir the mixture well and let it cool to lukewarm.

While the liquid mixture is cooling, mix flour, brown sugar, baking powder, salt, vanilla, and eggs into the butterscotch mixture; mix well. Fold in marshmallows and chocolate morsels.

Spread batter into a lightly greased 9x13 inch pan. Bake 25 minutes. Be careful not to overcook.

Easy Cheesecake Brownies

Ingredients

1 (19.8 ounce) package brownie mix

1 (8 ounce) package cream cheese

1 egg

1/3 cup white sugar

Directions

Prepare the brownie mix as directed by manufacturer. Preheat oven to temperature indicated on box. Grease a 9x13 inch pan.

Spread the brownie batter evenly into the prepared pan. Using an electric mixer, beat together the cream cheese, egg and sugar until smooth. Dollop the cream cheese mixture on top of the brownie batter. Swirl together using a knife or skewer.

Bake according to manufacturer's instructions. Brownies will be done when a toothpick inserted comes out clean. Cool in the pan, then cut into bars and serve.

Butterscotch Blondies

Ingredients
1 (18.25 ounce) package yellow cake mix with pudding

1/3 cup butter or margarine, softened

3 eggs, divided

1 cup chopped pecans, toasted

1 cup butterscotch-flavored chips

1 (14 ounce) can sweetened condensed milk

1 teaspoon vanilla extract

Directions
Preheat oven to 350 F. In large bowl, beat cake mix, butter and 1 egg at medium speed until crumbly.

Press evenly into greased 13x9-inch baking pan. Bake 15 minutes. Remove from oven; sprinkle with pecans and butterscotch chips.

In small bowl, beat sweetened condensed milk, remaining 2 eggs and vanilla. Pour evenly over chips.

Bake 25 to 30 minutes longer or until center is set. Cool thoroughly. Cut into bars. Store covered at room temperature.

Chocolate Mint Brownies

Ingredients

1 cup white sugar

1/2 cup butter, softened

1 (16 ounce) can chocolate syrup

4 eggs

1 teaspoon vanilla extract

1/2 teaspoon salt

1 cup all-purpose flour

2 1/2 cups confectioners' sugar

1/2 cup butter, melted

3 tablespoons creme de menthe liqueur

1 cup semisweet chocolate chips

6 tablespoons butter

Directions

Preheat oven to 325 degrees F (165 degrees C). Grease a 9x13 inch baking pan.

In a large bowl, mix together 1 cup of white sugar and 1/2 cup of butter until smooth. Beat in the eggs one at a time, then stir in the vanilla and chocolate syrup.

Combine the salt and flour; mix into the batter just until blended. Spread the batter evenly in the prepared pan.

Bake for 25 minutes in the preheated oven, until the brownies begin to pull away from the sides of the pan. Let cool.

In a medium bowl, mix together 1/2 cup melted butter and confectioners' sugar until smooth. Stir in creme de menthe liqueur. Spread over the cooled brownies and allow to cool completely.

Combine the chocolate chips and remaining butter in a microwave safe dish. Heat for 1 minute in the microwave, stir, then continue to heat at 30 second intervals, stirring each time, until melted and smooth.

Spread over the top of the brownies. Allow to cool completely before cutting into 2 inch squares.

Vanilla Brownies

Ingredients

2 1/4 cups all-purpose flour

2 1/2 teaspoons baking powder

1/2 teaspoon salt

3/4 cup unsalted butter, softened

1 1/4 cups white sugar

1 1/4 cups packed brown sugar

1 teaspoon vanilla extract

3 eggs

2 cups semisweet chocolate chips

Directions

Preheat oven to 350 degrees F (175 degrees C). Grease a 10x15 inch jellyroll pan.

In a small bowl, combine flour, baking powder, and salt. Set aside. In a large bowl, cream together the butter, white sugar, brown sugar, and vanilla until smooth.

Beat in the eggs, one at a time, then stir in the flour mixture. Mix in chocolate chips, if desired. Spread the batter evenly into the prepared pan.

Bake for 35 to 45 minutes in preheated oven. Cool in the pan on a wire rack. When completely cooled, cut into squares.

Double Chocolate Chip Brownies

Ingredients

2 cups (12-ounce package) Semi-Sweet Chocolate Morsels - divided use

1/2 cup butter or margarine, cut into pieces

3 large eggs

1 1/4 cups all-purpose flour

1 cup granulated sugar

1 teaspoon vanilla extract

1/4 teaspoon baking soda

1/2 cup chopped nuts

Directions

Preheat oven to 350°F (175°C). Grease a 13x9x2-inch baking pan.

Melt 1 cup morsels and butter in large, heavy-duty saucepan over low heat; stir until smooth. Remove from heat. Stir in eggs. Stir in flour, sugar, vanilla extract and baking soda. Stir in remaining morsels and nuts. Spread into prepared baking pan.

Bake for 18 to 22 minutes or until wooden pick inserted in center comes out slightly sticky. Cool completely in pan on wire rack.

Peppermint Brownies

Ingredients

1 1/2 cups margarine

3 cups white sugar

1 tablespoon vanilla extract

5 eggs

2 cups all-purpose flour

1 cup unsweetened cocoa powder

1 teaspoon baking powder

1 teaspoon salt

24 small peppermint patties

Directions

Mix butter, sugar, and vanilla. Beat in eggs till well blended. Stir in flour, cocoa, baking powder, and salt. Blend well.

Reserve 2 cups of batter, set aside

Grease 13x9x2 inch pan. Spread remaining batter in prepared pan. Arrange peppermint patties in a single layer over batter about 1/2 inch apart.

Spread reserved 2 cups batter over patties. Bake 350 degrees F (175 degrees C) for 50-55 minutes until brownies begin to pull away from sides of pan. Cool completely in pan on wire rack.

Walnut Chocolate Brownies

Ingredients

1 cup butter

4 (1 ounce) squares unsweetened chocolate

2 cups white sugar

3 eggs

1 teaspoon vanilla extract

1 cup all-purpose flour

1 1/2 cups chopped walnuts

1 cup semisweet chocolate chips

Directions

Melt butter and 4 squares unsweetened chocolate in a medium size saucepan over moderate heat. Remove from heat.

Preheat oven to 350 degrees F (175 degrees C).

Beat in sugar gradually with a wooden spoon until thoroughly combined. Add eggs, one at a time, beating well after each addition; stir in vanilla. Stir in flour until thoroughly combined. Stir 1 cup of the walnuts.

Spread into greased 13 x 9 x 2 inch pan. Combine remaining 1/2 cup walnuts with chocolate chips; sprinkle over top of brownie mixture, pressing down lightly.

Bake in a preheated oven for 35 minutes or until top springs back when lightly pressed with fingertip.

Cool completely in pan on wire rack. Cut into bars or squares.

Cherry Cheesecake Brownies

Ingredients

1 (16-ounce) can dark sweet cherries

1 (15-ounce) package brownie mix

2 large eggs - divided use

1/4 cup vegetable oil

1 (3-ounce) package cream cheese, softened

2 tablespoons granulate sugar

3/4 cup sweetened flaked coconut

1 teaspoon almond extract

Directions

Drain cherries, reserving 1/4 cup cherry juice. Put brownie mix in a large bowl. Add 1 egg, oil and reserved cherry juice; mix well. Gently stir in cherries. Set aside.

Put cream cheese and sugar in a medium mixing bowl. Beat with an electric mixer 3 to 4 minutes or until well mixed. Add remaining egg; mix well. Stir in coconut and almond extract.

Lightly grease an 8x8x2-inch baking pan. Spoon brownie mixture evenly into pan. Spoon cream cheese mixture over brownie mixture. Use a knife to swirl cream cheese mixture into brownie mixture.

Bake brownies in a preheated 350°F (175°C) oven 35 to 40 minutes, or until a wooden pick inserted near center comes out clean.

Let cool before cutting into squares or bars.

Coconut Brownies

Ingredients

1 cup butter, softened

2 cups white sugar

4 eggs

1 1/2 teaspoons vanilla extract

2 cups all-purpose flour

3/4 teaspoon cream of tartar

1/2 cup unsweetened cocoa powder

1/2 cup chopped walnuts

4 cups unsweetened flaked coconut

1 (14 ounce) can sweetened condensed milk

1 tablespoon vanilla extract

Directions

Preheat oven to 350 degrees F (175 degrees C). Grease and flour a 9x13 inch baking pan.

In a large bowl, cream together the butter and sugar. Beat in the eggs, one at a time, then stir in 1 1/2 teaspoons vanilla. Combine the flour, cream of tartar and cocoa; stir into the egg mixture until well blended. Fold in walnuts. Spread half of this mixture into the bottom of the prepared pan.

Make the middle layer. In a medium bowl, stir together the coconut, sweetened condensed milk and 1 tablespoon vanilla. Carefully layer this over the chocolate layer in the pan. Top with the remaining chocolate batter. Spread to cover evenly.

Bake for 45 to 50 minutes in the preheated oven, until top is no longer shiny. Cool in the pan before cutting into bars.

Coffee Brownies

Ingredients

2 pounds milk chocolate chips

1/4 cup instant coffee granules

1 cup unsalted butter, softened

2 cups white sugar

8 eggs

3 tablespoons vanilla extract

1 teaspoon ground cinnamon

1 teaspoon salt

2 cups all-purpose flour

Directions
Preheat the oven to 375 degrees F (190 degrees C). Grease and flour four 8x8-inch baking pans.

Place the chocolate chips and the coffee granules in a double boiler over simmering water. Cook over medium heat, stirring occasionally, until melted and smooth. Set aside.

In a large bowl, cream the butter and sugar together until light and fluffy. Beat in the eggs two at a time, mixing well after each addition. Stir in vanilla, cinnamon, and salt, then mix in the melted chocolate. Mix in flour until just blended. Divide the batter equally into the prepared pans, and spread smooth.

Bake for 35 minutes in preheated oven, or until the edges pull from the sides of the pans. Cool on a wire rack. Cover, and refrigerate for 8 hours. Cut the cold brownies into bars to serve.

Snickerdoodle Brownies

Ingredients

2 2/3 cups all-purpose flour

2 teaspoons baking powder

1 teaspoon salt

2 cups packed brown sugar

1 cup butter, softened

2 eggs

1 tablespoon vanilla extract

Topping:

2 tablespoons white sugar

2 tablespoons ground cinnamon

1/8 teaspoon ground ginger

Glaze:

1 cup confectioners' sugar

1/4 cup heavy whipping cream

1 tablespoon ground cinnamon

1 teaspoon vanilla extract

Directions

Preheat oven to 350 F (175 degrees C). Grease a 9x13-inch baking pan.

Whisk flour, baking powder, and salt together in a bowl. Beat brown sugar, butter, eggs, and 1 tablespoon vanilla extract together in a bowl using an electric mixer until smooth and creamy.

Stir flour mixture into creamed butter mixture until batter is well combined and thick; spread into the prepared baking pan.

Combine white sugar, 2 tablespoons cinnamon, and ginger together in a bowl; sprinkle over batter.

Bake in the preheated oven until blondies are beginning to pull away from the sides of the pan and are set in the middle, 25 to 30 minutes. Allow blondies to cool, at least 30 minutes.

Beat confectioners' sugar, cream, 1 tablespoon cinnamon, and 1 teaspoon vanilla extract together in a bowl until glaze is smooth; drizzle onto blondies.

Coconut Cherry Brownies

Ingredients

1/2 cup brown sugar, firmly packed

1/4 cup butter or margarine, softened

1 1/2 cups biscuit baking mix

2 large eggs

1/2 cup granulated sugar

1/4 teaspoon almond extract

1 cup coconut, flaked

1/2 cup almond, chopped

3 tablespoons biscuit baking mix

1/4 cup maraschino cherry, chopped

Directions

Preheat oven to 350°F (175°C).

Cream together brown sugar and softened butter. Stir in 1 1/2 cups biscuit baking mix.

Press in an ungreased 13x9x2-inch baking pan. Bake for 12 minutes.

Meanwhile, beat eggs in a medium bowl then mix in sugar and almond extract. Stir in flaked coconut, chopped almonds, and 3 tablespoons biscuit baking mix. Spread over the baked mixture.

Arrange chopped maraschino cherries on top.

Bake until light golden brown, about 20 to 25 minutes. Cool before cutting.

Dark Chocolate Brownies

Ingredients

1 2/3 cups (10 ounce package) dark chocolate morsels - divided use

1 cup granulated sugar

1/3 cup butter, cut into pieces

2 tablespoons water

2 large eggs

1 teaspoon vanilla extract

3/4 cup all-purpose flour

1/4 teaspoon salt

1/2 cup chopped walnuts or pecans

Directions

Preheat oven to 325°F (160°C). Grease 8-inch-square baking pan. Set aside 1/3 cup morsels.

Heat 1 1/3 cups morsels, sugar, butter and water in small saucepan over low heat, stirring constantly, until chocolate and butter are melted. Pour into medium bowl.

Stir in eggs, one at a time, with wire whisk until blended. Stir in vanilla extract. Add flour and salt; stir well. Stir in remaining 1/3 cup morsels and nuts. Pour into prepared baking pan.

Bake for 38 to 40 minutes or until wooden pick inserted in center comes out slightly sticky. Cool in pan on wire rack. Cut into bars.

Macadamia Nut Brownies

Ingredients

1/2 cup butter

3 ounces unsweetened baking chocolate

1 cup granulated sugar

2 large eggs

1 teaspoon vanilla extract

3/4 cup all-purpose flour

1/4 teaspoon baking powder

1/4 teaspoon salt

1 1/4 cups chopped toasted macadamia nuts - divided use

Directions

Preheat oven to 350°F (175°C). Butter an 8-inch square pan.

In a medium-sized saucepan, melt butter and chocolate together over very low heat, stirring occasionally. Remove from heat and transfer to mixing bowl.

Beat in sugar, eggs and vanilla until smooth and creamy. Blend in flour, baking powder and salt until just blended. Fold in 1 cup of the nuts.

Spread mixture in pan. Sprinkle top evenly with remaining 1/4 cup of nuts. Bake 20 to 25 minutes. Do not overbake; center should be set, but still moist. Cool completely in pan on wire rack. Cut into squares.

Raspberry Walnut Brownies

Ingredients

4 (1-ounce each) squares unsweetened baking chocolate

1/2 cup vegetable shortening

3 large eggs

1 1/2 cups granulated sugar

2 1/2 teaspoons vanilla extract

1/4 teaspoon salt

1 cup all-purpose flour

1 1/2 cups chopped walnuts

1/3 cup raspberry jam

2 tablespoons butter

2 tablespoons light corn syrup

1 cup powdered sugar

1 tablespoon milk

Directions

Preheat oven to 325°F (160°C). Grease an 8-inch square pan; set aside.

In the top of a double boiler over warm water, melt 3 squares baking chocolate with shortening. Cool slightly.

In a bowl beat eggs, sugar, 1 1/2 teaspoon vanilla, and salt. Stir in the chocolate mixture and flour. Beat till thoroughly combined. Stir in chopped walnuts.

Pour batter into prepared pan.

Bake for 40 minutes. Remove from oven and immediately spoon raspberry jam over the hot brownies. Cool completely on a wire rack.

For Chocolate Glaze: Melt 1 square baking chocolate; blend in butter and light corn syrup. Stir in powdered sugar, milk, and 1 teaspoon vanilla. Beat till thoroughly combined.

Drizzle glaze on top of cooled brownies. Cut into bars.

Printed in Great Britain
by Amazon